THE STORY OF
SELENA
QUINTANILLA

A Biography Book for New Readers

—— Written by ——
Gloria Arjona

—— Illustrated by ——
Juanita Londoño

ROCKRIDGE PRESS

This book is dedicated to the memory of Selena Quintanilla-Pérez, and to all the underrepresented groups who, like her, face structural, economical, educational, gender, and racial barriers.

CONTENTS

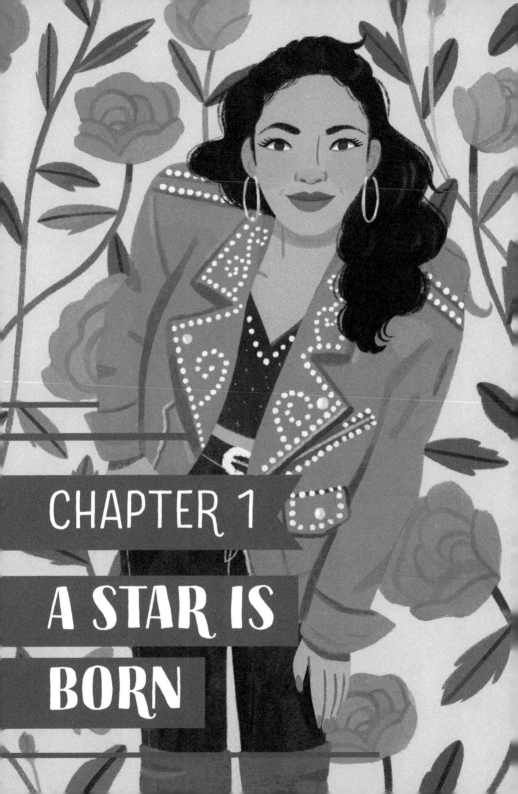

CHAPTER 1

A STAR IS BORN

Meet Selena Quintanilla

When Abraham and Marcella Quintanilla (kin-tah-NEE-ya) went to the hospital to have their third child, they thought he would be a boy named Marc Anthony. They did not have a name ready when a girl was born instead! Marcella's hospital roommate suggested the name Selena. Mr. Quintanilla repeated "Seh-LEH-na?" No, "Seh-LEE-na," the roommate insisted, waking up the baby. Little Selena cried loudly. Everybody was surprised that a five-pound baby could make so much noise. A star was born!

By age eight, Selena, who had taken no music lessons, was already known as "the girl with the big voice." She became the queen of **Tejano** (teh-HAH-noh) music, a Spanish-language music style from Texas and northern Mexico.

Before Selena's success, Tejano singers were mostly men. At age fifteen, she became the

WHERE?

TEXAS

MEXICO

LAKE JACKSON

youngest female singer to win a Tejano Music Award. She became a role model for Mexican American children and other young people of color. Selena grew up in an **underprivileged** family, and her success proved what she always said, "The impossible is always possible."

Selena made sacrifices to be a famous musician. She rehearsed her songs and dance moves for hours. She barely ever went out to play. She even had to stop attending school and finished her education by mail. When she became famous, she often visited schools to encourage kids to study and to remind them that school is a privilege.

Selena changed the Tejano music world by including women and by adding **cumbia** and **disco** to her singing—and also lots of glitter to her clothes.

3

Selena's World

Selena Quintanilla was born on April 16, 1971, in Lake Jackson, Texas. Her mom, Marcella, and her dad, Abraham (also called Abe), were Mexican-American—Americans with a Mexican background.

Selena's mom loved to cook **Tex-Mex food**, like quesadillas with cheddar cheese. Selena loved

nachos with melted yellow cheese, but her favorite food was pizza!

Selena heard Spanish spoken at home, especially when family members were expressing their feelings. Selena's mom called Selena *m'ijita* (mee-HEE-tah) or my dear daughter. But English was the language the family used most. As a child, Selena's dad had been punished in school for speaking Spanish. He did not want that treatment for his children.

Selena could not speak Spanish well, but she could sing in Spanish. It wasn't until later, when she became famous and started traveling to Mexico often, that she decided to study Spanish. At first, she was frustrated because she understood more than she could say, and she tended to mix both languages. She had difficulty rolling her *r*'s, an important sound in the

Spanish language. But Selena was a determined and very proud Mexican-American. After much work, she became 100 percent bilingual.

> " I didn't have the **opportunity** to learn Spanish when I was a girl, but it's **never too late** to get in touch with your **roots.** "

WHEN?

Texas becomes an American state.	Abraham Quintanilla is born in Corpus Christi, TX.	Selena is born in Lake Jackson, TX.
1845	**1939**	**1971**

CHAPTER 2

THE EARLY YEARS

Making Music

Selena had music in her blood. Her dad had been in a band called Los Dinos in 1957, when he was a teenager. He left the band when he and Marcella married. He needed a stable job. But music was his joy, and his children were talented.

Selena's dad started teaching her older brother, Abraham (known as A.B.), how to play bass guitar. Meanwhile, Selena would pretend to read her dad's music books and sing whatever songs she wanted. At just eight years old, her voice was already powerful. Her pitch and rhythm were perfect, and she had **charisma**. Abe decided that Selena would have her own band. He called the new band Southern Pearl. Selena sang, Abe played guitar, A.B. played the bass guitar, and Selena's older sister, Suzette, played the drums. Selena's mom made the band's outfits and taught Selena how to make them, too.

The band practiced every day. Soon Southern Pearl sounded great. People started asking the band to play music at their parties and clubs. Abe thought that some of the bars and clubs were not appropriate for Selena. He and Marcella opened a Tex-Mex restaurant called Papagayo's, where Marcella cooked and Southern Pearl played music.

Selena was happy. She had her own band and a place to perform. Selena loved to sing "Feelings" by Morris Albert and other popular songs in English. Unfortunately, customers at Papagayo's were expecting to hear songs in Spanish.

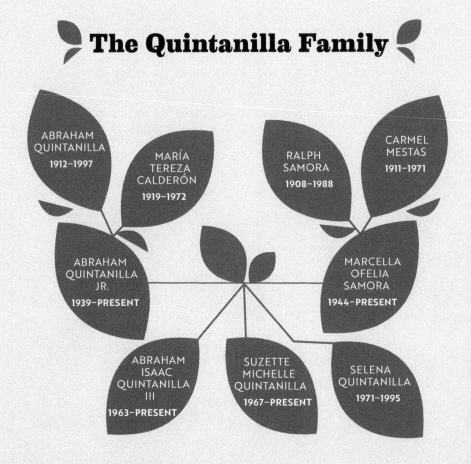

The Quintanilla Family

ABRAHAM QUINTANILLA
1912–1997

MARÍA TEREZA CALDERÓN
1919–1972

RALPH SAMORA
1908–1988

CARMEL MESTAS
1911–1971

ABRAHAM QUINTANILLA JR.
1939–PRESENT

MARCELLA OFELIA SAMORA
1944–PRESENT

ABRAHAM ISAAC QUINTANILLA III
1963–PRESENT

SUZETTE MICHELLE QUINTANILLA
1967–PRESENT

SELENA QUINTANILLA
1971–1995

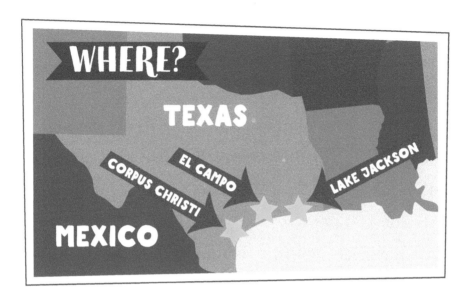

A New City

In 1980, when Selena was nine, the Quintanillas were losing money. They had to close Papagayo's. They also lost their home. Selena's uncle lent the family an old trailer for them to live in at El Campo, where Selena finished fifth grade. They lived there for one year and then moved to Corpus Christi.

Corpus Christi is a big city where a lot of Selena's extended family lived. Some of Abe's old friends were now music **producers**. Selena missed the beautiful trees of Lake Jackson, but she was serious about music. Corpus Christi could mean more opportunities.

From Friday to Sunday, Southern Pearl played at weddings, **quinceañeras** (KEENS-ah-NYAIR-uhs), and festivals. Sometimes Selena missed school, and her teachers were concerned. But she never got behind. Selena knew how to study by herself.

Southern Pearl was a good band, but the **gigs** they got were not great. People were not enthusiastic about their music. One day, Abe saw

an animated crowd dancing to the beat of a Tejano music band. He was amazed to see how everyone, Mexicans and non-Mexicans, were dancing together. The next morning, he announced to the family that there was no more Southern Pearl. Then their father added that they would now be Selena y Los Dinos (Selena and the Dinos), a Tejano music band, and that they would sing songs in Spanish.

JUMP
—IN THE—
THINK TANK

Without understanding the words of a song, what are some other things you might enjoy about it? Do you enjoy music in other languages?

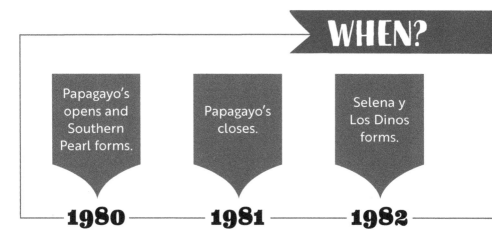

WHEN?

Papagayo's opens and Southern Pearl forms.	Papagayo's closes.	Selena y Los Dinos forms.
1980	**1981**	**1982**

CHAPTER 3
SELENA Y LOS DINOS

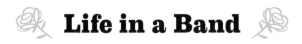 Life in a Band

Selena, A.B., and Suzette were happy to still be playing together in a band, but they didn't like Tejano music very much. Selena wanted to sing pop songs in English. Her dad explained that people in Corpus Christi loved dancing, and Tejano music was easy to dance to. But Selena didn't even know how to speak Spanish. Abe promised to teach her.

Selena learned many Spanish songs. She liked them. She also found that her dad had been right—people in Corpus Christi loved these songs. Selena y Los Dinos played in local clubs and at fairs.

The name of the band began to spread around Texas. But there was a problem—Selena was missing school. Her reading teacher, Ms. Greer, told Abe that even though Selena's grades

JUMP
-IN THE-
THINK
TANK

Are math and science more important to learn than arts? What are your favorite subjects?

were excellent, music was not as important as other subjects. Abe disagreed. He believed music was an important part of Selena's education. He took Selena out of school, and starting in eighth grade, she was homeschooled instead.

Selena studied every day. She spent most of her time singing, going to radio and TV interviews, and recording. In her small amount of free time, she made drawings of the fancy clothes she hoped to have one day.

In 1984, Selena released her first album, *Selena y Los Dinos*. She was only thirteen years old, but her popularity was growing fast. The band was also growing. Two new members joined in 1985—Ricky Vela played the keyboard and Roger García played guitar. Selena was

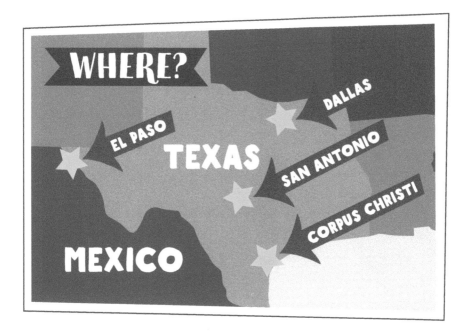

happy to have them, but she still felt lonely sometimes. All her bandmates were older than her!

 Big Bertha

Selena y Los Dinos traveled to San Antonio, Dallas, El Paso, and other cities with large Spanish-speaking populations. To save on travel costs, Abe bought a tour bus. They called it Big

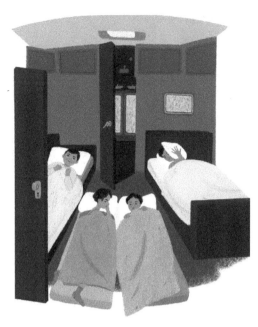

Bertha. From the outside, it was a nice band bus. Inside, it was not fancy at all. The seats were old. There were no bunk beds. They all had to sleep together on the floor, in their sleeping bags. There was no air conditioning or heating. It was freezing in the winter and hot in the summer. Big Bertha was not perfect, but now Selena had a place to sit and draw new clothing designs.

There were now five members of Selena y Los Dinos, but Selena was the star. She won awards and recognitions by herself. In 1984, when she was thirteen, she was nominated for Female Vocalist of the Year at the Tejano Music Awards. The next year, they also nominated her

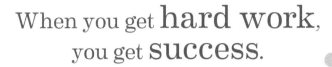

> When you get **hard work**,
> you get **success**.

for Female Entertainer of the Year and Female
Vocalist of the Year. In 1986, her single *"Dame un
Beso"* (DAH-meh oon BEH-soh) or "Give Me a
Kiss" became a hit, a very popular song. She was
invited to perform
on a popular
Spanish TV show,
*The Johnny Canales
Show*. She had sung
on the show when
she was thirteen,
but now she was
a fifteen-year-old
who could finally
speak Spanish.
To look older,

Selena cut her hair very short and wore makeup and jewelry. Johnny was impressed by how quickly Selena had learned Spanish. Her charm and beauty were also impressive. Her star was starting to shine!

WHEN?

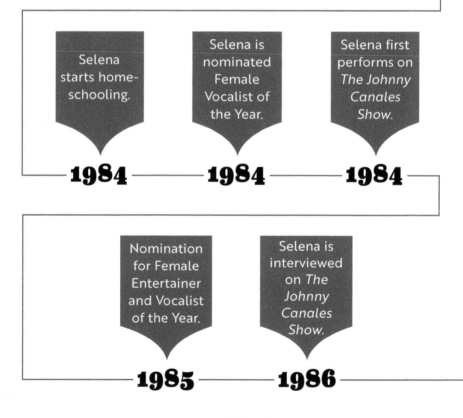

Selena starts home-schooling.

Selena is nominated Female Vocalist of the Year.

Selena first performs on *The Johnny Canales Show.*

1984 — **1984** — **1984**

Nomination for Female Entertainer and Vocalist of the Year.

Selena is interviewed on *The Johnny Canales Show.*

1985 — **1986**

CHAPTER 4
EXCITING CHANGES

# Proving Herself

Selena saw that the world of Tejano music was a man's world. Her dad explained that Tejano music was named after Mexican cowboys and other Mexican and Spanish settlers. They wouldn't think a girl like Selena could be a Tejano singer. But Selena and her dad knew that they were wrong.

Selena knew that girls could do the same things anyone else did. Her sister, Suzette, was an example. She was a drummer, even though most drummers they knew were men. Selena would be a **Tejana** in her own way. She designed

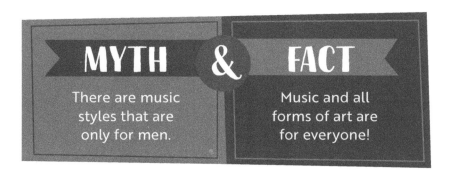

MYTH & FACT	
There are music styles that are only for men.	Music and all forms of art are for everyone!

a traditional **mariachi**-style jacket in a vibrant purple satin fabric, something nobody had done before. This jacket would become Selena's **signature** look.

With Selena, Tejano music became fancy. Many Mexican-American girls who never liked this music before came to Selena's concerts wearing flashy **bolero jackets**.

Selena's popularity surprised some producers who thought that Tejano music could not be performed by women. There was only one well-known Tejano woman singer—Laura Canales, known as the Queen of the Tejano Wave. Selena admired Laura. She never imagined that soon she would be the new queen of Tejano.

That day came at the 1986 Tejano Music
Awards, when Selena was nominated Female
Vocalist of the Year. Everybody thought that
Laura would be the winner, not a 15-year-old
girl! When Selena won, she was surprised.
Selena realized that she was accomplishing
something big. And she was right. Many more
awards would come.

A New Band Member

Selena y Los Dinos performed in different cities
every day. Roger, the guitar player, had recently
married and had to quit the band in the middle
of a tour. A.B., who was now responsible for
writing Selena's songs and getting the band's
gigs, panicked. They had a concert in just a few
days! He searched for another guitar player
all over San Antonio. Finally, he found a very
skillful guitar player. His name was Chris Pérez.
Although Chris didn't normally play Tejano

music, he knew about Selena y Los Dinos. He accepted A.B.'s invitation to meet them the next day.

When Chris arrived at the rehearsal, Abe didn't like his long hair. Selena thought that Chris was cute. They all agreed that he was a great guitar player. Chris became one of Los Dinos.

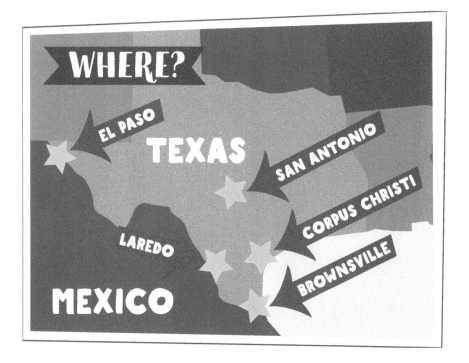

Do you think
that very
different
people can
get along
well? How
would you
describe
yourself?

Selena y Los Dinos now spent most of the time on the road. They played together, they slept on the floor of Big Bertha, and they ate together every day. Selena and Chris became very close. They had many things in common, even though they were different. Selena was lively and social. Chris was shy and quiet.

Selena liked to talk. Chris enjoyed listening to her. Selena and Chris fell in love. They started a romantic relationship, but decided to keep it a secret. They knew that Abe would not accept that Selena had a boyfriend. Abe would always tell her that having a boyfriend would distract her from her music. But Selena didn't think so. Music was as important to Chris as it was to Selena.

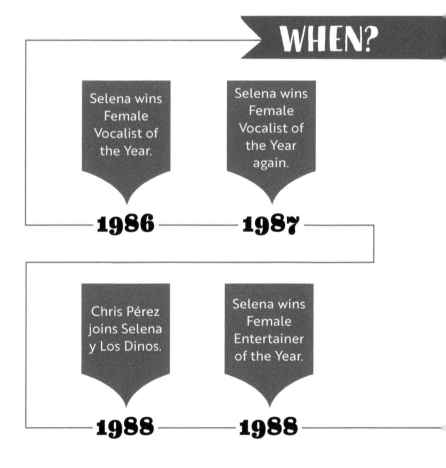

WHEN?

Selena wins Female Vocalist of the Year.

Selena wins Female Vocalist of the Year again.

1986 — **1987**

Chris Pérez joins Selena y Los Dinos.

Selena wins Female Entertainer of the Year.

1988 — **1988**

CHAPTER 5

A RISING STAR

New Opportunities

After producing five albums over four years, in 1988 Selena y Los Dinos released two more albums: *Preciosa* (preh-SYOH-sah) or *Pretty Girl* and *Dulce Amor* (DOOL-seh ah-MOHR) or *Sweet Love*. Selena became the most requested Tejano singer on the radio. The same year, Selena won Female Entertainer of the Year at the Tejano Music Awards for the first time. She holds the world record for most wins in this category. In 1989, she was awarded both Female Vocalist and Female Entertainer of the Year.

José Behar, head of the Latin Music Division of the record company EMI, saw Selena performing. He wanted to help make Selena an international celebrity. José promised her that after being successful in Latin America, she would **cross over** into the English market. There was one condition that Selena didn't like—even though Los Dinos

JUMP
—IN THE—
THINK TANK

Why do you think a high school diploma was so important for Selena? How can a diploma change a person's life?

would record with her, only her name would be on the album cover. After she discussed this with A.B. and Suzette, they told her it was okay with them, so Selena decided to record the album. Selena's first solo album was released as *Selena*. She changed her look from previous albums. Her hairstyle, jewelry, and clothing changed. The album was a big success!

Selena placed number seven on the **Billboard Regional Mexican Albums** chart and led to Selena winning again both Female Vocalist and Female Entertainer of the Year at the

 I don't feel **pressure**, because I'm not trying to portray something that I'm not.

1990 Tejano Music Awards. It also helped spread **Selenamania** to Latin America!

That year, another important accomplishment for Selena arrived in the mail: her high school diploma. Selena was thrilled. She wanted everyone to know that not only did she have a beautiful voice, but she was an intelligent and hardworking student, too.

 Choosing Her Own Path

In the midst of her rising fame, Selena caught the attention of Coca-Cola. They thought that she was perfect to represent Coke in

Latin America. For Selena, it was a great opportunity. She signed a contract with them. A.B. and Chris wrote a tune for Selena's Coke commercial that sounded like one of her songs.

Selena's love for Chris grew with her fame. Soon she would be twenty-one. Her family still didn't know about their relationship, so she decided to secretly marry him. It was a simple ceremony in Nueces County in Texas, with only Selena, Chris, and the judge. But Selena was too famous to have secrets. When they left the courthouse, some radio stations were already talking about her marriage. Selena's dad was furious. Selena's mom calmed him, and soon he accepted Chris as part of the family. Selena's dad

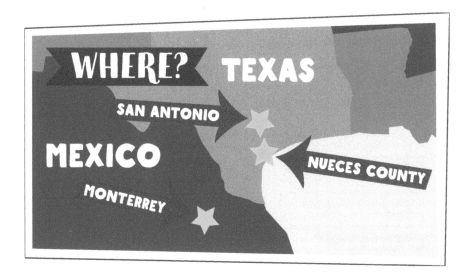

WHERE? TEXAS

SAN ANTONIO

MEXICO

MONTERREY

NUECES COUNTY

bought Selena and Chris a house next door to
him and Selena's mother.

Selena's life was full of love, music, and tours.
Her album *Entre a Mi Mundo* (EHN-treh ah mee
MOON-doh) or *Enter My World* was a hit in Latin
America. José planned an international tour for
her. The first city was Monterrey, Mexico.

Selena was nervous when she saw the
reporters waiting to interview her in Spanish.
But she was brave and honest. She did her best.
When she forgot a Spanish word, she smiled.

People of Monterrey loved Selena's **modesty** and charm. Newspapers said only good things about this beautiful Tejana who seemed to be proud of her humble origins and her Mexican heritage. Newspapers called her "an artist of the people."

WHEN?

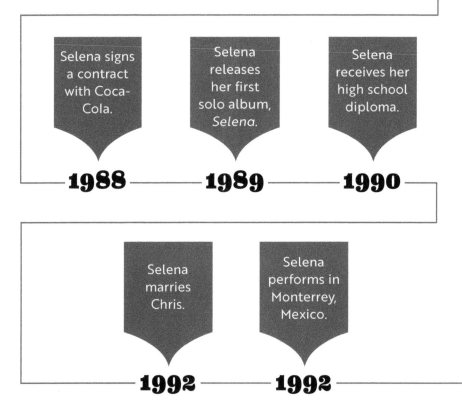

Selena signs a contract with Coca-Cola.

Selena releases her first solo album, *Selena.*

Selena receives her high school diploma.

1988 —— **1989** —— **1990**

Selena marries Chris.

Selena performs in Monterrey, Mexico.

1992 —— **1992**

CHAPTER 6

DREAMS COME TRUE

🌹 Selena the Designer 🌹

In 1994, another of Selena's dreams came true. She opened a boutique and salon called Selena Etc. in Corpus Christi, TX. With the help of a professional designer, Martin Gómez, the designs that Selena had been working on while touring became a reality. People rushed to buy belts, earrings, and jackets designed by Selena. Everybody was surprised by her business success, except her mom. Marcella knew how serious Selena was about fashion and all the years she planned for this moment. Selena often explained, "I want to do something outside the music business to see whether I'm *un poquito inteligente*" (oon poh-KEE-toh een-teh-lee-HEHN-teh) or "a little bit intelligent." Selena Etc. was so successful that in only a few months she opened another shop in San Antonio, TX.

Selena's shops kept her very busy. She had recordings, shows, interviews, and volunteer work, and she wanted to spend time with Chris. On top of everything, Selena's fans were in the thousands now, and she loved to be in touch with them. Selena hired a friend of the family to take care of the fans and to help with the shops. Although Selena still stayed involved with her business, she could now pay the most attention to her music career.

 ## Selena Live!

Selena was now an international star. In 1993, she performed in Nuevo León, Mexico, for an audience of 70,000 people, making her the

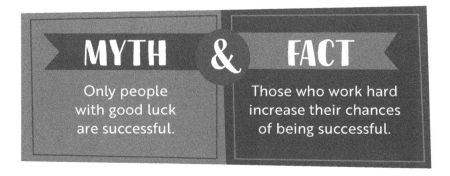

MYTH & FACT

Only people with good luck are successful.

Those who work hard increase their chances of being successful.

biggest Tejano act in Mexico. Televisa, the
largest media company in Mexico, gave her a
role in their successful soap opera *Dos Mujeres,
un Camino* (dohs moo-HEH-rehs, oon kah-MEE-
noh) or *Two Women, One Road*.

Back in Corpus Christi, Selena played a
fan-packed concert at the Memorial Coliseum.
It was recorded and later turned into the album
Selena Live. Selena was awarded Female Vocalist

and Female Entertainer of the Year for the fifth year in a row, and her album *Entre a Mi Mundo* won awards at both the Tejano Music Awards and **Lo Nuestro Awards**. Then Selena signed a contract with her record company to distribute her music worldwide. Her dream to cross over was becoming a reality!

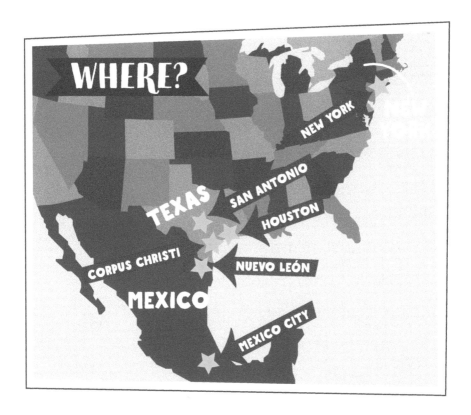

JUMP
—IN THE—
THINK TANK

How do you think Selena felt when she received the Grammy? Have you ever received an award? How did you feel?

In 1994, Selena traveled to New York City for the Grammy Awards, the most important award show in the music business. There was a **rumor** that *Selena Live* might win best Mexican-American album. Selena thought that this was just gossip. No Tejano woman singer had ever received a Grammy. When she heard the announcer say, "and the Grammy goes to . . . *Selena Live!*" Selena was in shock! She was so nervous that she was afraid she might fall on her way to the stage.

40

Selena took a deep breath and slowly walked to the stage, where she graciously received the award and thanked everyone. In her long glittering white dress, Selena was a queen!

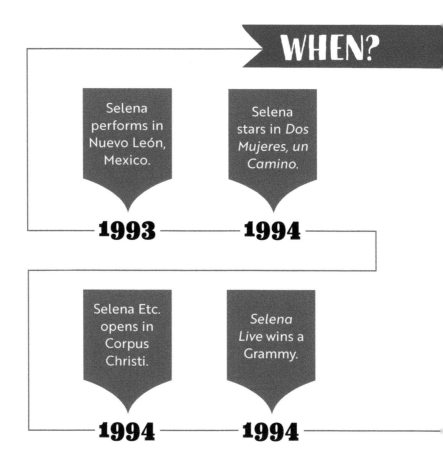

WHEN?

Selena performs in Nuevo León, Mexico.

Selena stars in *Dos Mujeres, un Camino.*

1993 —— **1994**

Selena Etc. opens in Corpus Christi.

Selena Live wins a Grammy.

1994 —— **1994**

CHAPTER 7

THE QUEEN OF TEJANO

Breaking Records

In 1994, Selena performed at the Festival Acapulco in Guerrero, Mexico. There she was declared queen of the festival. Back in Texas, she gave a concert near her hometown, Lake Jackson. Abe saw a girl in the audience who was blind and told Selena. Selena came to meet the young fan, Maricela, and gave her a big hug. Maricela almost cried tears of joy. This made Selena really happy. No matter how famous she got, Selena loved connecting with her fans.

Selena's album *Amor Prohibido* (ah-MOHR proy-BEE-doh) or *Forbidden Love* was released that year. It was a mix of Tejano, cumbia, rock, and **ranchera** music styles.

JUMP
–IN THE–
THINK TANK

Why do you think Maricela almost cried tears of joy? How can people cry when they are not sad?

There was a new song written by Selena, with a title she invented to mimic the sound of the heart of people in love: "Bidi Bidi Bom Bom." The album was a hit—and not just with people in Texas. In Southern California, where Tejano music was not popular, people loved it. Selena immediately placed at the top of *Billboard* magazine's Latin and Mexican Regional chart. It became a **platinum album** four times over.

New opportunities opened for Selena. She had a special appearance as a ranchera singer in the movie *Don Juan DeMarco*. Selena toured in Los Angeles, New York, Puerto Rico, El Salvador, and Guatemala. She had a memorable concert at the Astrodome in Houston, where more than 60,000 people saw her circling the arena in a horse-drawn carriage. Selena wore a gorgeous

purple suit that she designed. The magazine
Texas Monthly named her one of the twenty most
important Texans of 1994.

 Selena's Legacy

In early 1995, Selena gave a concert in Chicago,
gathering Spanish and English speakers

together. She was recording *Dreaming of You,* a new album with English and Spanish songs.

Unfortunately, in March 1995, Selena was killed by a troubled friend. The news of Selena's death devastated her family and fans around the world. Thousands of people placed flowers and candles outside of Selena Etc. stores.

Dreaming of You was released a few months later. On its first day, 175,000 copies were sold, making it the bestselling Latin album in the United States and making Selena the first Latin solo artist to reach number one on the *Billboard* top albums chart.

Soon Hollywood wanted to make a film of Selena's life. But who would play Selena?

> " I want to be **remembered** not only as an entertainer but as a person who **cared a lot**. And I gave **the best** that I could. "

Thousands of women auditioned, among them Jennifer Lopez, a Puerto Rican singer and actress. Jennifer studied everything about Selena—her singing, her laughter, and her dance. She won the role. The film *Selena* launched Jennifer's career and opened the doors for other **Latinx** (lah-TEE-neks) actors.

Today, Selena's memory is still alive. There are books about her, including one by her husband, Chris Pérez. In Corpus Christi, there is a Selena Museum, a memorial statue, and the *Fiesta de la Flor* (FYEHS-ta deh lah flohr) or Flower Festival.

Her name is in the Texas Women's Hall of Fame, and her birthday was declared Selena Day in Texas. Selena has a star on the Hollywood Walk of Fame, and in 2020 Netflix released an original series about Selena's life.

WHEN?

Amor Prohibido is released.

Selena performs at the Astrodome.

Selena dies on March 31.

1994 — **1995** — **1995**

The film *Selena* is released.

Netflix releases *Selena: The Series.*

1997 — **2020**

CHAPTER 8

SO ... WHO WAS SELENA QUINTANILLA

?

Challenge Accepted!

Now that you know so much about Selena's life and work, let's test your new knowledge in a little who, what, when, where, why, and how quiz. Feel free to look back in the text to find the answers if you need to, but try to remember first.

1 Where was Selena born?

→ A New York, New York
→ B Lake Jackson, Texas
→ C Monterrey, Mexico
→ D Corpus Christi, Texas

2 Who taught Selena how to sing?

→ A A private music teacher
→ B Her sister, Suzette
→ C Herself
→ D Her schoolteacher

3 **What kind of songs did Selena love to sing as a child?**

→ A   Tejano songs in Spanish

→ B   Children's songs

→ C   Traditional bilingual songs

→ D   Pop songs in English like "Feelings"

4 **To what big city in Texas did the Quintanillas move when Selena was a child, becoming important for her music career?**

→ A   Corpus Christi

→ B   San Antonio

→ C   Austin

→ D   El Paso

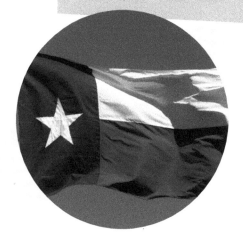

5 **Why were Selena y Los Dinos unsuccessful in their first gigs in Corpus Christi?**

→ A   People in Texas loved quiet music.

→ B   People wanted to hear only English songs.

→ C   People didn't like Selena's voice.

→ D   People wanted music to dance to.

6 **When did Selena learn proper Spanish?**

→ A   When she was a baby

→ B   When she was eight years old

→ C   As a teenager, when she was already a Tejano singer

→ D   She never learned to speak Spanish

7 **Why was it hard for Selena to make it as a Tejano singer?**

→ A   There were already too many women Tejano singers.

→ B   Tejano singers were mostly men, and much older than Selena.

→ C   Selena was too old to be a Tejano singer.

→ D   Selena's voice was not strong.

8 **What did Selena love to do besides singing?**

→ A   She loved to cook and eat pizza.

→ B   She loved to play the piano.

→ C   She loved to design clothing.

→ D   She loved to ride her bike.

9 **Why was it important for Selena to have her high school diploma?**

→ A   She believed in education.

→ B   To show that she had brains in addion to a beautiful voice.

→ C   She wanted to be a good role model.

→ D   All of the above.

10 **Why is Selena considered a role model?**

→ A   She sang songs in English and Spanish.

→ B   Young people of color can identify with her.

→ C   She had a lot of money.

→ D   She was beautiful and talented.

 Our World

Selena's life was short, but it had a positive impact in many ways. Look at a few things that are now different because of Selena.

→ The great success of her album *Dreaming of You* made it easier for other Spanish-language singers to cross over into the English market, including Ricky Martin and Shakira. As a successful female singer in a male-dominated Tejano world, Selena influenced younger female American singers like Ashlee Simpson, Beyoncé, and Lady Gaga, who have all spoken about being inspired by Selena's style and career.

→ Latin music in the United States continues to evolve thanks to Selena and her brother, A.B., who blended the traditional Tejano music with a wide range of Caribbean rhythms, disco, and pop. By winning a Grammy for best Mexican-American album with *Selena Live*, Selena raised the status of Spanish-language music in the United States.

→ Selena continues to be a major source of inspiration for creative women of color. Before Selena, most successful Latinas on TV were white and came from rich families. Selena proudly displayed her dark hair and skin, and never hid the fact that her parents were poor and lacked a formal education.

JUMP
—IN THE—
THINK
TANK
FOR

MORE!

Let's think a little bit more about what Selena did as a person and as a performer, and how her music and her actions changed our world.

→ How has Selena's music success in the United States paved the way for other singers?

→ How do Selena's many accomplishments motivate you?

→ How does Selena's determination to be always proud of who she was inspire others? How does it inspire you?

Glossary

Billboard Regional Mexican Albums: A chart listing the bestselling albums in regional Mexican music genres, published by the American music magazine *Billboard*

bolero jacket: A short, tailored jacket inspired by jackets worn by Spanish bullfighters

charisma: Especially strong personal charm

cross over: To succeed as an artist in a language market other than one's own

cumbia: A music style created in Colombia, popular in much of Latin America

disco: An American music style popular in the 1970s with a steady dancing beat and electronic sounds

gig: A paid performance

Latinx: Someone of Latin-American heritage; sometimes "Latino" is used for men and "Latina" for women

Lo Nuestro Awards: Meaning "Our Thing," Spanish-language awards show honoring Latin music

mariachi: A Mexican folk band traditionally formed by men elegantly dressed in black outfits inspired by Spanish bullfighting clothes

m'ijita: Spanish expression meaning "my dear daughter"

modesty: Being humble

platinum album: An album that has sold one million copies

producer: A person who helps an artist make music

quinceañera: Spanish term for a girl who turns fifteen. In the United States, it refers to a girl's fifteenth birthday celebration.

ranchera: Traditional Mexican music named after the ranch lands where it was first performed

rumor: A story going around that might not be true

Selenamania: Excitement about Selena, her music, and her style

signature: Closely associated with a certain person, as with a distinctive mark or characteristic

Tejana: A woman native of Texas with Mexican heritage

Tejano: A man native of Texas with Mexican heritage, or the music style named after them

Tex-Mex food: Mexican-American food often served in southern Texas

underprivileged: Having fewer advantages than others

Bibliography

Biography.com Editors. "Selena Quintanilla Biography." Biography. Last modified October 8, 2021. biography.com/musician/selena.

Cummins, Mary. "Family Tree of Selena Quintanilla." Geneastar. Accessed September 15, 2021. en.geneastar.org/genealogy /quintanilla/selena-quintanilla.

Medina Mora, Katina, and Hiromi Kamata, directors. *Selena: The Series*, created by Moisés Zamora. Netflix, December 4, 2020 to May 4, 2021.

Miracle, Jean. "Curiosidades del Nuevo Álbum De Selena Quintanilla" (Curiosities of the New Selena Quintanilla Album). Selfanaticos Online, YouTube. Accessed October 28, 2021. youtube.com/watch?v=DSgxOvmqh14.

Nava, Gregory, director. *Selena*. Warner Bros., 1997.

Paredez, Deborah. *Selenidad*. Durham, NC: Duke University Press, 2009.

Patoski, Joe Nick. *Selena: Como La Flor*. Boston: Little, Brown, 1996.

Acknowledgments

Selena Quintanilla first caught my attention while being interviewed by Mexican actress Verónica Castro. Selena's eyes and skin were brown. Her Spanish was not the one spoken by the privileged, but by those with a long history of educational deprivation. Nevertheless, Selena taught us that we all have the potential to succeed. Thanks to those who keep Selena's memory alive through videos, look-alike contests, tributes, books, and festivals. Special thanks to the editors and staff of Callisto Media for their initiative to honor Selena.

About the Author

GLORIA ARJONA teaches Spanish at the California Institute of Technology and has translated Hispanic authors. She is the author of *Posadas Unknown Calaveras* (Floricanto Press, 2020) and *¡Lotería!* (Floricanto Press, 2020). She has a passion for music. She sings and plays the guitar as part of her multimedia storytelling series, through which she aims to empower underrepresented communities. Learn more at GloriaArjona.com.

About the Illustrator

JUANITA LONDOÑO is a children's book, editorial, and commercial illustrator from Medellín, Colombia. She has a degree in animation concept art from the Vancouver Film School. She has worked for clients like Simon & Schuster, HarperCollins, Target, American Greetings, and Quarto. She likes drawing characters and environments with vibrant colors and textured details.

WHO WILL INSPIRE YOU NEXT?

EXPLORE A WORLD OF HEROES AND ROLE MODELS IN
THE STORY OF... BIOGRAPHY SERIES FOR NEW READERS.

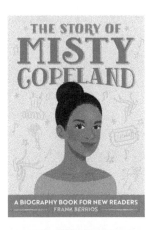

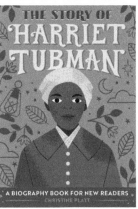

LOOK FOR THIS SERIES
WHEREVER BOOKS AND EBOOKS ARE SOLD

Alexander Hamilton

Albert Einstein

Martin Luther King Jr.

George Washington

Jane Goodall

Barack Obama

Helen Keller

Marie Curie

CPSIA information can be obtained
at www.ICGtesting.com
Printed in the USA
JSHW061418150922
30453JS00003B/8